Name

Phone

Email

Other journals from GOLDING NOTEBOOKS | *My Spirit Animals*

My Spirit Animal: Hedgehog Journal

6" x 9", 110 Pages, Standard B&W Lined

ISBN: 9781726880596

See the wide-ranging collection of
GOLDING NOTEBOOKS
now available on Amazon

/   /

／ ／

/ /

/   /

/ /

/ /

/ /

／　／

/ /

Made in the USA
Middletown, DE
08 March 2019